"The Disciplines of Devotion series is a timely and valuable resource for women who long to grow in spiritual depth and maturity. With biblical insight and godly wisdom, each volume offers practical help for cultivating habits that lead us closer to Christ. I'm thankful for this series and eager to see how God will use it to strengthen and encourage the hearts of women."

Melissa B. Kruger, author; Vice President of Discipleship Programming, The Gospel Coalition

"These gospel-centered primers are saturated with scriptures that nourish the delight of knowing Christ. The accessible content, coupled with practical ideas and heart-oriented application questions, invites the reader to draw near to God through cultivating Spirit-empowered holy habits."

Karen Hodge, Coordinator of Women's Ministries, Presbyterian Church in America; coauthor, *Transformed: Life-Taker to Life-Giver* and *Life-Giving Leadership*

Fasting

Disciplines of Devotion

Edited by Winfree Brisley

Fasting, by Cassie Achermann

Prayer, by Courtney Reissig

Sabbath Rest, by Megan Hill

Fasting

Cassie Achermann

WHEATON, ILLINOIS

Fasting

Published by Crossway
1300 Crescent Street
Wheaton, Illinois 60187

Cover design: David Fassett

Cover image: Getty Images and Rawpixel

First printing 2026

Printed in the United States of America

Trade paperback ISBN: 979-8-8749-0376-3
ePub ISBN: 979-8-8749-0378-7
PDF ISBN: 979-8-8749-0377-0

Library of Congress Cataloging-in-Publication Data

Names: Achermann, Cassie, 1994– author.
Title: Fasting / Cassie Achermann.
Description: Wheaton, Illinois : Crossway, 2026 | Series: Disciplines of devotion | Includes bibliographical references.
Identifiers: LCCN 2025004028 (print) | LCCN 2025004029 (ebook) | ISBN 9798874903763 (trade paperback) | ISBN 9798874903770 (pdf) | ISBN 9798874903787 (epub)
Subjects: LCSH: Fasting—Religious aspects—Christianity. | Fasting—Biblical teaching. | Spiritual life—Christianity.
Classification: LCC BV5055 .W377 2026 (print) | LCC BV5055 (ebook) | DDC 248.4/7—dc23/eng/20250825
LC record available at https://lccn.loc.gov/2025004028
LC ebook record available at https://lccn.loc.gov/2025004029

Crossway is a publishing ministry of Good News Publishers.

BP 35 34 33 32 31 30 29 28 27 26
15 14 13 12 11 10 9 8 7 6 5 4 3 2 1

For my parents, Peter and Linda Watson,
who first taught me to hunger for the Lord.

Contents

Series Preface

ON A CHILLY JANUARY MORNING, two friends and I huddled around a coffee shop table to share life updates and prayer requests. One friend reflected on the previous year with frustration: "I feel like I didn't accomplish anything." The other friend and I, surprised by her assessment, rattled off a long list of worthwhile things she had done. But she persisted. It wasn't that she truly believed she had accomplished nothing; it was that the things she had done weren't the things she had hoped to do. Things she valued had been pushed aside by what seemed more urgent in the moment.

I could say the same, and I bet you could too. As women living in a do-it-all culture, we tend to have a lot on our plates. We juggle work, husbands, children, aging parents, and friends. We manage households, serve in the church, and volunteer in the community. Year after year, many of our goals and good intentions get pushed to the back burner—especially when it comes to spiritual growth.

We want to grow in relationship with the Lord. We want to know the Bible better, fight sin, and establish a consistent prayer life. But amid all the things we have to do, we often miss the one thing we really need. In Psalm 27:4 David said,

> One thing have I asked of the LORD,
> that will I seek after:
> that I may dwell in the house of the LORD
> all the days of my life,
> to gaze upon the beauty of the LORD
> and to inquire in his temple.

As king, David surely had many things to do and many things he might have asked of God. But he knew that what he most needed was to dwell with the Lord. Similarly, Jesus explained to Martha in Luke 10:41–42 that she was "anxious and troubled about many things, but onc thing is necessary." What was the one thing? Sitting at his feet, listening to his teaching.

As you consider your relationship with the Lord, are you more like David or Martha? Are you *devoted* or *distracted*? I suspect that many of us would admit that we identify with Martha's distraction but also long for David's devotion. So how can we grow in devotion to God in a world of endless distractions?

We see from both David and Martha that a life devoted to the Lord won't happen by accident. David resolved to seek after God's presence. Jesus suggested that Martha needed to sit down and listen. You see, discipline helps us grow in devotion.

In fact, throughout history Christians have used spiritual disciplines such as prayer, fasting, and Bible study to seek the Lord and grow in relationship with him. If the phrase "spiritual disciplines" sounds intimidating, don't worry! It simply means practices that promote spiritual growth.[1] And these practices can help you draw near to God whether you're a new believer or have been walking with the Lord for decades.

Perhaps the idea of cultivating a life of devotion to the Lord is new or confusing, and you don't know where to start. You have faith in Christ, but you're trying to figure out what it looks like to grow in relationship with him.

Or maybe you're going through the motions of spending time with God, but if you're honest, he feels distant. You want the Holy Spirit to warm your affections for the things of God and restore the joy of your salvation.

Or perhaps you have a vibrant relationship with the Lord, but you'd like to learn new ways to seek him. You've been wanting to try fasting or you'd like to learn about Sabbath rest.

Whatever your situation, the Disciplines of Devotion series was written for you. Each booklet explores

1 Donald S. Whitney, *Spiritual Disciplines for the Christian Life* (NavPress, 1991), 17.

one thing—one practice to cultivate, one spiritual discipline to grow in—to help you draw near to the one true God. In each booklet, you'll gain a biblical understanding of a particular discipline and why it's worth cultivating. And you'll explore three practical ways to get started.

If you'd like to grow in these disciplines alongside other believers, we've included reflection questions to facilitate group discussion. Consider using this series in one-on-one discipleship, with a group of teens, in a neighborhood Bible study, or with a church small group. Also, Christians have a variety of perspectives on these disciplines, so if you'd like to continue your personal study, you can find a list of recommended resources at the end of each booklet.

When you finish this volume, let me encourage you not to set it aside in a pile of good intentions. These booklets can be read in less than an hour, but the disciplines they recommend can help you seek the Lord for a lifetime—even as you go about all the things you have to do.

Preaching about the "one thing" David desired in Psalm 27:4, Scottish pastor Alexander Maclaren observed, "Most of us seem, to our own consciousness, to live amidst endless distractions all our days. . . . But if we are true to the one purpose of serving and keeping near God, then we have a charm against the frittering away of our lives in distractions."[2]

The Disciplines of Devotion series isn't about productivity or efficiency or doing less. It's about pursuing a life of devotion to the Lord in an age of endless distraction. It's an invitation to "taste and see that the LORD is good!" (Ps. 34:8) no matter how much is on your plate.

Winfree Brisley
SERIES EDITOR

2 Alexander Maclaren, *Expositions of Holy Scripture: Psalms* (Eerdmans, 1932), 146.

1

What Is Fasting?

I USED TO WISH I could eat toast for every meal. Toast with peanut butter. Toast with Vegemite (an Aústralian classic). Occasionally, the sweet delight of toast with jam. I wanted to live on carbs.

But as the years have passed and I've left my twenties behind, my body has let me know I need vegetables. Lunchtime has increasingly featured soups in the winter and salads in the summer. And to my surprise, my appetite for healthier foods has grown (though I still love my morning toast). I sometimes even look forward to loading up my salad bowl.

Our spiritual appetites need a similar recalibration so that we find pleasure in Christ instead of in the world's offerings.

We look for satisfaction in the next swipe of the credit card, the next glowing report about our kids, the next career milestone, or the next hundred Instagram followers. Yet contentment eludes us time and time again. The solution isn't to continue pursuing the sugar rushes of what this world can offer but to seek what truly nourishes.

The practice of fasting can be part of this recalibration because it helps us draw near to God. Our famished souls learn that there's no one more satisfying than him. If you're worn out trying to capture elusive joy in this world, join me as we explore how fasting can give you the only hunger that leads to lasting satiation.

What Is Fasting?

In my early teens, I did World Vision's 40 Hour Famine a few times with my sisters, which meant going without food to raise money for people facing poverty.[1] We'd wander around church clutching our sponsorship books, and kind folks who knew I was shy would take pity on me and offer to donate.

When the designated weekend came, we'd lay at home groaning for what felt like endless hours while our dad intentionally wafted his food aromas in our direction. As soon as the clock struck noon on Sunday, we'd rush to McDonald's and down triple-cheeseburger meals.

Until a couple of years ago, the 40 Hour Famine was my only fasting experience (apart from some blood tests). But these periods of white-knuckle deprivation and constant complaining are a far cry from biblical fasting. They had a different purpose—to raise awareness and money rather than to help me spiritually.

In contrast, the kind of fasting we consider in this booklet refers to going without food for a limited time to aid prayer. Let's consider each part of this definition.

Fasting is *going without food*. People fast from things other than food, such as social media or

1 For more information, see https://40hourfamine.com.au/.

television. Those fasts can be beneficial and may be your only option if you can't fast for medical reasons.[2] I hope this booklet is helpful for those cases, but our focus is only on abstaining from food (going without water for a fast of any length is dangerous).

Fasting is practiced *for a limited time*. The goal of fasting isn't to go as long as you can without food. It's not meant to be a continual state of life. Food is a good gift from God, and most of the time we're to enjoy it with thanksgiving (1 Tim. 4:4; cf. 1 Cor. 10:31). After all, there is "a time for every matter under heaven" (Eccl. 3:1)—a time to fast and a time to feast.

Fasting *aids prayer*. We're not talking about fasting for medical reasons, as a weight-loss strategy, or even as a mere exercise in self-control. It's always a God-ward practice done for the Lord and by his strength.

2 If you have any medical conditions that may make fasting inadvisable, talk to your doctor first. Those with eating disorders will likely find fasting more harmful than helpful. Those with a history of eating disorders should likewise exercise caution and seek godly counsel. Remember, fasting is an aid, not a requirement. You're no less godly if wisdom dictates that you shouldn't participate.

Don't think of fasting as a burdensome task to add to your already overflowing to-do list—it is rather a means of helping you bring all your neediness and weakness to God's throne.

I began fasting out of a sense of deep need for God. A Bible study I had worked through left me yearning for God to bring revival in my heart as well as in my church.[3] I started small, skipping lunch once a week and instead spending that half hour praying. Not long after, I added a second day in the week. These weren't aimless, wandering prayer times; I was asking the Lord urgently for help in two specific areas: first, for a breakthrough in an area of ongoing sin, and second, for spiritual revival in my church, where I'd been facing discouragement and difficulty for a while.

I've never regretted a time of fasting. It has pushed me toward heartfelt prayer more than almost anything else in my life. Any pain and discomfort has been worth it for renewed closeness to the Lord.

3 Nancy DeMoss Wolgemuth and Tim Grissom, *Seeking Him: Experiencing the Joy of Personal Revival* (Moody Publishers, 2019).

I haven't always received the specific outcome I've wanted, but even when my situation hasn't changed, my heart has.

Fasting in the Bible

God's people have fasted in all kinds of ways throughout history. We dig into some passages in more detail later in this booklet. For now, let's briefly tour the Bible to see why God's people fasted.

Obeying God's Command

There's only one instance in the Bible where God commanded people to regularly fast. Under the old covenant law, Israel was to observe the Day of Atonement once a year. They gave offerings, abstained from work, and "afflicted" themselves (Lev. 23:26–32), meaning they fasted.[4] This demonstrated how serious their sins were and how much they needed God's mercy. It was an outward sign of inward humility, and the whole nation was to do this together.

4 John Currid, notes on Leviticus, in *ESV Study Bible* (Crossway, 2008), 239.

Believers under the new covenant do not observe the Day of Atonement, given that Christ fulfilled what it foreshadowed in his death. But the principle behind it resonates with the example of others in Scripture who fasted, inviting us to continue the practice today.

Expressing Repentance and Grief

Fasting in the Old Testament was often a sign of mourning, particularly for sin. One notable example is in the book of Jonah. God instructed the reluctant prophet to go to the wicked city of Nineveh and announce its impending destruction. Jonah was reluctant, but he eventually obeyed. Surprisingly, the people of Nineveh didn't just mourn what was coming to them but mourned their sin. They put on sackcloth, wept, and fasted as a display of genuine repentance (Jonah 3:5–9). And God relented from destroying them (v. 10).

Throughout the Old Testament, people expressed grief over their sin or the sins of others through fasting and prayer.[5]

5 For example, see 1 Sam. 7:6; 1 Kings 21:20–29; Ezra 9:1–5; Neh. 1; Dan. 9:1–19.

Seeking God's Protection, Provision, or Guidance

Expressing repentance often involved petition—people asked God for mercy or deliverance from the consequences of sin. But there are also many passages where fasting served to intensify other requests.

In the book of Esther, the Jews faced eradication under the king's edict. Only Esther could persuade the king to change his mind, but she could be killed for coming before him unbidden. She called on all the Jews to join her in fasting for three days and three nights (Est. 4:15–16). Though it's never explicitly stated, this fasting would have been accompanied by prayer.[6] By God's miraculous hand, the king was favorable toward Esther, and the Jews were spared.

God's people also fasted and prayed for deliverance in battle, protection while traveling, guidance for decisions, fulfillment of the Lord's promises, and more.[7]

6 Wallace P. Benn, *Ezra, Nehemiah, and Esther: Restoring the Church*, Preaching the Word (Crossway, 2021), 163.

7 For example, see Judg. 20:26; 2 Chron. 20:3–4; Ezra 8:21–23; Luke 2:36–38.

Jesus on Fasting

Fasting continued in the New Testament, even after Jesus's arrival. Jesus fasted for forty days and forty nights in the wilderness before he was tested by Satan.[8] When the evil one tried to convince Jesus to turn a stone into bread, using his divine power to serve his own interests, Jesus quoted Scripture and gave us what may be the key attitude for fasting: "Man shall not live by bread alone" (Matt. 4:4). Going without food reminds us that there is something more important and satisfying than food.

Jesus also explicitly taught his followers about fasting. In the Sermon on the Mount, he instructed them not to fast to impress others (Matt. 6:16–18). He condemned those who boasted in their fasting before God as if it made them righteous (Luke 18:10–14).

8 Jesus's forty-day fast paralleled Moses's fasts (see Ex. 34:27–28; Deut. 9:18–19) and the Israelites' wandering in the wilderness for forty years (Deut. 8:2). This was a special period when Jesus proved himself as God's obedient Son. God preserved both Jesus and Moses, as his representatives, beyond what a human being can normally handle. So these examples aren't normative for us.

In Matthew 9:14–15, Jesus spoke about the right time to fast. He was questioned by John the Baptist's disciples about why his own disciples didn't join the customary fasts. His answer implied that the Jews had forgotten what fasting was meant for. Jesus, the bridegroom, was bodily present with his people. Fasting with Christ made as little sense as mourning at a wedding celebration. One day, he said, they would fast again, when he was taken away from them at his ascension. The church did this in the first century (Acts 13:1–3; 14:23). In other words, Jesus's disciples didn't need to fast because he was physically present with them. Fasting is helpful for us, however, because we're physically separated from our Lord and long for him to return.

Across the Old and New Testaments, God's people have fasted. And Christians have continued ever since. You might see your needs reflected in these biblical stories. Do you feel weighed down by your sin, grieved by evil in the church or world, or desperate for God's presence and guidance? Though fasting doesn't seem common in evangelical circles today, many throughout history have followed the example of the early church and the rest of the biblical witness. Might you join them?

Reflection Questions

1. What experience do you have with fasting, if any? (It could be fasting from certain types of food, social media, etc.)

2. What sparked your interest in fasting or led you to read this booklet?

3. What did you learn from the biblical examples of fasting in this chapter? Which one most resonated with you?

2

What Are the Blessings of Fasting?

MY DAD HAS BEEN A RUNNER for over a decade—he has completed more than sixty marathons, and he even ran the whole length of New Zealand solo in two months. I had always thought he was crazy, and I claimed I'd never take up running. With all the exhaustion and injuries he has endured, surely the payoff couldn't be worth the pain.

He got the shock of his life when I announced I'd started a Couch to 5K training plan.

I didn't suddenly find it easy. Even now that I'm in the habit of running a few times a week, it's still painful. But I don't merely know of running's benefits; I've experienced them firsthand. It gives me more energy, it clears my head, and it strengthens my body. I'm enjoying being able to push myself after a decade of chronic illness.

You may have the same doubts about fasting as I did about running. It's uncomfortable. It goes against what our bodies want. But despite the cost—even because of the cost—fasting is a means that God uses to bless us. The payoff is worth it.

Fasting Is Neglected

When you think about spiritual disciplines, Bible reading and prayer probably come to mind first. We know we should practice these, and innumerable books help us do them better. But fasting? Not so much. We rarely see it taught on, written about, or modeled. You might not intentionally choose to skip fasting; it just doesn't occur to you in the first place.

You're not alone. Despite the biblical evidence for fasting's relevance, it's an overlooked spiritual discipline. Before we consider the benefits, let's look at a couple of roadblocks. Why is this discipline so rarely practiced among Christians today?

It's Uncomfortable

While we can read our Bibles with a coffee mug in hand and a fuzzy blanket on our knees, fasting doesn't inspire images of comfort and coziness. In a decadent society that prizes self-reliance, productivity, and following our desires, it seems crazy to empty ourselves of strength and deny what our senses cry out for.

It's Misunderstood

If you do encounter people fasting, it probably doesn't seem like something for *you*. Surely fasting is for isolated monks. Or for extreme John-the-Baptist types. If anyone in our church fasts, we put her in the "super Christian" box. Fasting must be for someone with exemplary self-control who has mastered the faith basics and is looking to level up.

Fasting Is Worth It

When we misunderstand fasting and how to honor God in it, we'll avoid it altogether. That's why we need to see it from Scripture's perspective.

By stripping away the comforts our culture tells us are essential, we see that they're only cheap imitations of God's comfort. Fasting isn't reserved for those with great self-control; it's also for those who see their need for self-control. It's not reserved for those who walk closely with God; it's also for those who lament their distance from him. If you're tired of relying on yourself, if you've experienced the emptiness of worldly comforts, if you desire a deeper relationship with God—fasting is for you.

And fasting is worth it. Here are a few blessings that come from this practice.

We Commune with God

Seeing more of God is the central benefit of fasting. Isn't it why we practice spiritual disciplines in the first place? To come nearer to Christ, to draw strength and joy from his presence? As this booklet series explores, these practices help us cultivate disciplines of devotion so we can focus on the one thing we desperately need: to "dwell in the house of the Lord" and to "gaze upon [his] beauty" (Ps. 27:4). If every other gift of fasting fell away, this would be enough.

Fasting helps us see more of God because it facilitates our communion with him through prayer. That's why John Piper calls it the "humble, hungry handmaid of faith" that prompts us to pray.[1] Fasting is pointless when not paired with talking to God—it's an empty ritual, a form of self-deprivation to show our mettle.

Consider Paul's warnings against both trying to obtain righteousness by abstention and treating the body severely (Col. 2:20–23; 1 Tim. 4:1–4). Some claim that these verses teach against fasting altogether. But as we saw from the early church's example, fasting is a fitting response to longing for Christ's return (Matt. 9:15). Our goal in fasting is

1 John Piper, *A Hunger for God: Desiring God Through Fasting and Prayer* (Crossway, 1997), 64.

to commune with God, not to earn his approval or secure our own salvation. While fasting does help us teach our bodies that they're not our masters, that's not the main purpose. Our focus should be less on what we're saying *no* to and more on the better *yes* in its place. All the benefits of fasting are downstream from this one: deepening our relationship with God through prayer.

Let's consider a few ways that fasting does this.

We See Ourselves Rightly

I can give many reasons why my prayer life isn't as vibrant as I want: I'm busy. There's so much ministry to do. I haven't found the right system. But Nick Thompson unmasks the reality: "Where prayer is wanting, humility is wanting."[2] My lack of felt dependence keeps me from praying. I don't feel as though I need it.

Fasting doesn't make me weak and dependent—it reveals how weak and dependent I've been all

2 Nick Thompson, *Growing Downward: The Path to Christ-Exalting Humility* (Reformation Heritage, 2022), 140.

along. When I feel the piercing hunger pangs, I'm reminded how quickly my body breaks down without food that God provides daily. He's the source of everything I need for life: food, water, oxygen, and shelter. So I'm drawn to him in dependent praise and gratitude.

When I feel capable, I'm more likely to *work* instead of *pray*. I can maintain the illusion of self-sufficiency. Fasting reorients me to the reality of my creatureliness and casts me on my Creator.

We Love What's Worthy

When food is taken away, we realize how much we've relied on it for satisfaction and comfort. For those like me who struggle with emotional overeating, this absence is especially revealing—all this time, I've been turning to a gift instead of to the giver.

Without food as an easily accessible crutch, I have to look elsewhere. In *Habits of Grace*, David Mathis writes, "In that gnawing discomfort of growing hunger is the engine of fasting, generating the reminder to bend our longings for food godward and inspire intensified longings for Jesus."[3]

Fasting creates space so that I can turn to Christ with my boredom, my anxiety, and my desire for control and find that "my soul [is] satisfied as with fat and rich food" (Ps. 63:5). I hunger less for food and more for righteousness—and for the righteous one (cf. Matt. 5:6).

As we sharpen our affections for Christ through fasting,[4] our longing to see him face-to-face grows. Fasting is a temporary measure because the bridegroom is coming back (Matt. 9:14–15; John 14:1–3). Through our deprivation now, we're viscerally reminded to long for the right thing—not for the dinner we'll eat in a few hours but for the wedding feast of the Lamb and the fellowship we'll enjoy with him forever (Rev. 19:6–7). Fasting is an expression of longing for Christ's coming that in turn intensifies our longing.

3 David Mathis, *Habits of Grace: Enjoying Jesus Through the Spiritual Disciplines* (Crossway, 2016), 121.

4 Mathis, *Habits of Grace*, 117.

We See God Work

Prayer is communion with God, but it's also more than that. The Lord encourages us through Paul to bring all our requests and thanksgiving to him (Phil. 4:6). We come to God with our needs and desires, asking him to act in particular ways.

Fasting adds fuel to the fire of our prayers. It's similar to how the posture of kneeling helps orient our hearts toward the Lord. By "leaning into the lack," we feel our weakness bodily.[5] We come more desperately; we come with more faith. We get the joy of focusing all our neediness on the one who promises to provide for all our needs (Phil. 4:19).

We mustn't treat fasting like a formula: Subtract food and receive the answer we want. King David fasted and prayed for the life of his newborn son, but the boy died anyway (2 Sam. 12:15–23). Despite such a devastating outcome, David still worshiped the Lord (v. 20). Praising God even when our prayers

5 Justin Whitmel Earley, *The Common Rule: Habits of Purpose for an Age of Distraction* (InterVarsity Press, 2019), 130.

aren't answered the way we desire is an act of trust that his wisdom is greater than ours.

When answers are delayed, we still have reason for confident hope. In Luke 2:36–38, the elderly prophetess Anna spent her days in the temple worshiping, fasting, and praying as she awaited the promised Savior—and she lived long enough to give thanks to God as the baby Jesus was brought into the temple.

Remember the examples from the previous chapter: Believers fasted, and God heeded their prayers. If we humble ourselves and bring our requests to the Lord, he will answer according to his superior wisdom. We can use this God-given means of grace and trust that, whatever the outcome of our petitions, we'll benefit by learning to rely more on the Lord. That's his work too.

Throughout Scripture, believers have intensified their prayers with fasting in times of special need. Let's imitate them and see what God does. In the next few chapters, we consider what this looks like practically. I want to encourage you to fast with humility, fast with a plan, and fast with God's people—all for the joy of communing with God.

Reflection Questions

1. Why is it so important for fasting to be connected to prayer?

2. Which blessing of fasting is most compelling to you?

3

Fast with Humility

FEW ACTIVITIES TEST a relationship like assembling IKEA furniture—especially if one obsessively checks the instruction manual at every step while the other prefers to figure it out as they go along.

Me? I'm an instruction booklet girl all the way, and not only for the steps showing the right way to assemble the piece. I've also been saved by the diagrams covered with bold *X*'s showing you what *not* to do. Those warnings keep us from making mistakes that are difficult to fix later on.

The Bible likewise teaches us what not to do, presenting warnings alongside the examples of godly fasting. These show us how crucial it is to tend to our hearts as we take up disciplines such as fasting. We not only need to pray *as* we fast; we need to pray *about* our fasting, humbly asking the Lord to help us avoid these pitfalls.

Before we learn how to fast in the next chapter, let's consider how not to fast.

Avoid Presumption

After a lengthy season of weekly fasting, with no improvement in the situation, I sat dejected before a friend. "I've been praying and fasting about this for eight months," I said, "and somehow things are worse than ever."

Partly, this was weariness and discouragement talking—weakness rather than sin. But part of me felt as though God owed me a change in my situation since I'd prayed so hard for so long.

In Isaiah 58, we find a similar situation with God's people. They appeared godly on the surface—they apparently delighted in drawing near to God, they cried out in prayer, and they fasted.

But God knew the complaint they made in their hearts:

> Why have we fasted, and you see it not?
> Why have we humbled ourselves, and you
> take no knowledge of it? (v. 3)

You can hear the entitlement. They had fasted, so God was supposed to give them what they asked for. If they lived in our cultural context, they might dutifully read a Bible chapter every morning, give a percentage of their income to the church, and volunteer in three ministries. The Israelites trusted in the power of their actions, not the power of the one to whom they prayed.

When we fast, we can guard against this sort of presumption by remembering the gospel. Salvation is an undeserved, gracious gift from our loving heavenly Father. Fasting is not a bargaining chip we can use to convince him to respond in a particular way, like petulant children who hold their breath until their parents cave to their demands. We have already received the ultimate gracious gift in our salvation. Any other good thing is yet another unearned mercy from the Lord, including answered prayers. Rituals such as fasting or even Bible reading and church attendance cannot make us righteous or accumulate favor with the Lord to be cashed in later. We're justified by Christ alone. He gave those who trust in him the right to be called "children of God" (John 1:12), so we can boldly approach our Father with all our requests. Find your confidence to pray in his goodness and love, not in your actions or worthiness.

Avoid Hypocrisy

As we continue to read Isaiah 58, it's clear presumption wasn't the Israelites' only problem. God pierced through their outward piety and revealed what a true fast looks like:

> "Is such the fast that I choose,
> a day for a person to humble himself?
> Is it to bow down his head like a reed,

and to spread sackcloth and ashes under him?
Will you call this a fast,
and a day acceptable to the LORD?

"Is not this the fast that I choose:
to loose the bonds of wickedness,
to undo the straps of the yoke,
to let the oppressed go free,
and to break every yoke?" (vv. 5–6)

One commentator says the Israelites were "role-playing righteousness."[1] They performed outward rituals but failed to obey God's costlier commands. True humility, God told them, issues forth not in sackcloth and wailing and ashes but in open hands that are willing to share what they have.

If we have humbly accepted Jesus, he'll bring forth the fruit of righteous living and obedience in our lives. This shows that we truly know him. We cannot use fasting as a cover-up for continuing in sin or failing

1 Raymond C. Ortlund Jr., *Isaiah: God Saves Sinners*, Preaching the Word (Crossway, 2012), 387.

to care for the needy. As John Piper writes, "Woe to the fasting that leaves sin in our lives untouched."[2]

Avoid Boasting

Warnings about the dangers of fasting extend to the New Testament, including in the Sermon on the Mount. After warning against hypocritical showmanship in both giving and prayer, Jesus said,

> And when you fast, do not look gloomy like the hypocrites, for they disfigure their faces that their fasting may be seen by others. Truly, I say to you, they have received their reward. But when you fast, anoint your head and wash your face, that your fasting may not be seen by others but by your Father who is in secret. And your Father who sees in secret will reward you. (Matt. 6:16–18)

While Isaiah 58 revealed how the Israelites were trying to curry God's favor by their fasting, Jesus

2 John Piper, *A Hunger for God: Desiring God Through Fasting and Prayer* (Crossway, 1997), 135.

targeted the horizontal dimension: using fasting to impress other people.

As we've seen, God prescribed only one regular fast for his people on the Day of Atonement. Yet by Jesus's time, it had become customary among Jews to fast twice a week on Mondays and Thursdays.[3] Those who wanted to be seen as righteous would ensure that people knew they were following these fast days. They let their hunger and discomfort show on their faces. It was like when I did the 40 Hour Famine as a teenager—my complaints could be heard several neighborhoods away.

Jesus said people who fast in this way "have received their reward" (Matt. 6:16). The fleeting praise of others will be our only reward for hypocritical fasting; it will bring us no intimacy with Christ.

Embrace the Reward

We shouldn't conclude from these passages that fasting is to be discarded. For all Isaiah's warnings, there's

3 R. Kent Hughes, *Luke: That You May Know the Truth*, 2 vols. in 1, Preaching the Word (Crossway, 2014), 196.

good news too. God promises to hear those who fast with a pure heart and hands and who walk in righteousness:

> Then shall your light break forth like the dawn,
> and your healing shall spring up speedily;
> . . .
> Then you shall call, and the LORD will answer;
> you shall cry, and he will say, "Here I am."
> (Isa. 58:8–9)

And in Matthew 6, Jesus doesn't ban fasting but teaches us to do it the right way: secretly, humbly, and trusting in the reward that God will hear and heed us. Remember his promise: "Your Father who sees in secret will reward you" (v. 18).

Let these warnings make you more prayerful about your fasting, but don't let them discourage you from its reward for the purehearted. God *does* listen to his people's prayers—but he does so because of his mercy and generosity, not because of our outward ceremonies.

Reflection Questions

1. Of the three dangers of fasting presented in this chapter (presumption, hypocrisy, and boasting), which do you feel you're most likely to fall into? Why?

2. What steps can you take as you plan your fast to avoid this danger?

4

Fast with a Plan

NOW THAT YOU'VE SEEN the blessings of fasting and the reward held out to those who do it with a pure and humble heart, you may be eager to get started. But before you resolve to cut out your next three meals, let's plan and prepare well for a fast.

In this chapter, we consider how to plan your purpose, process, and rhythm in fasting.

Purpose

In a given fast, you could pray about any area where you sense a deep need for God. The following questions will help you search your heart before the Lord to discern where fasting may be beneficial:

- What areas of your life or character has God challenged you about recently through sermons at church (or through your Scripture reading, Bible studies, Christian books, or conversations with godly friends)?
- Read passages about the behavior we're called to put off and put on as Christians (e.g., Gal. 5:16–26; Col. 3:5–17). How is God prompting you to change?
- Do you feel stuck in battling any long-term sin patterns? How could you benefit from proactive prayer about these areas?
- What decisions are before you? Could you pray for God's guidance and wisdom about a job change, a move, a potential spouse, or a ministry direction?
- What situations are your loved ones facing that you want to regularly bring before God? Could you face the affliction of fasting to

suffer alongside someone enduring infertility, a prodigal child or spouse, mental health challenges, or a financial crisis?
- How has God particularly burdened your heart? Do you feel an urgency to take action against abortion, for the evangelization of the unreached, or for revival in your church, city, or nation?

Reflecting on these questions may have brought up so many needs that you feel overwhelmed. If so, let that drive you to God right now. Pray and ask him for wisdom on where to start and how fasting might put an edge on your petitions. God promises he will generously give us wisdom when we seek it from him (James 1:5).

Process

We've seen that fasting is a "handmaid," or help, for prayer.[1] Deprivation in itself isn't the point. So we

1 John Piper, *A Hunger for God: Desiring God Through Fasting and Prayer* (Crossway, 1997), 64.

should plan in advance how we'll use this special time of prayer.

It's hard for me to sit down and pray for an extended period without some structure or materials. My mind wanders easily. And if I'm praying about one specific issue, my petitions can circle round and round. If you also prefer more structure, consider these ideas to prepare for fasting and prayer:

- Make a list of Scripture passages to read and pray through that relate to your purpose for fasting.
- Use a binder or notebook to list the specific petitions you end up praying. The act of writing keeps me focused, and it's encouraging to look back through the pages and see God's answers to my prayers.
- Gather material to read and pray through. This could be devotional material that stirs your heart to love Jesus, putting you in a frame of dependence and gratitude. It could

> be books or articles about a specific issue that you read through and stop regularly to pray about and make personal. I often use the notes I've taken from books since those tend to be personally relevant points that have stuck out to me.

I also leave room for God's Spirit to guide me in prayer. He might direct me to Scripture passages I hadn't written down or bring something to mind that diverts me from my list. Prayer shouldn't be formulaic, but preparation can focus your prayer so it does more for your heart.

Rhythm

How long should you fast? And how often should you fast? Should you do it alone or with a group?

You may be frustrated that the Bible gives little practical guidance, but this is freeing. We aren't bound by rules; we can fast in whatever way cultivates our dependence on God. We can follow the Spirit's leading.

I don't want to prescribe certain approaches, but learning what I do may help you. Let's consider the length and timing of fasts, leaving the question of fasting with others for the next chapter.

How Long Should You Fast?

In Scripture, both Moses and Jesus fasted completely for forty days, but these aren't examples we're meant to imitate. They were unusually sustained by God as his representatives in special moments of redemptive history (see Ex. 34:28; Deut. 9:9, 18; Matt. 4:1–11). Other people in the Bible fasted for various lengths of time (we're usually not told how long).

I recommend starting small. I've never gone without food for more than twenty-four hours; often, I just skip one or two meals (though I'm open to longer fasts in the future). I spend what would have been a mealtime in focused prayer, and for the rest of the fast, I let the hunger pangs prompt me to make quick petitions. Remember that fasting should serve your prayer life, not showcase your endurance. Consider what rhythms will effectively "sharpen [your spirit], and enliven the powers of the soul" for the sake of prayer.[2]

How Often Should You Fast?

Consider various approaches to how often you fast. You can view fasting as a special measure for times of urgent need. Or it can be a regular practice among other spiritual disciplines that forms a normal part of your walk with God.

I take both approaches. I've had seasons when particular needs were pressing on me, and I knew a one-time prayer session wouldn't cut it. I needed to bring these issues regularly before God as the persistent widow did to the judge in Jesus's parable (Luke 18:1–8). So I set a weekly or twice-weekly time to fast for several months.

But there are also days when I've thought, "I need to fast tomorrow." I may feel spiritually apathetic, overly busy and stressed, or consumed by worldly pleasures. I crave to return to closeness with the Lord,

2 William Gurnall, *The Christian in Complete Armour* (Glasgow, 1865; facsimile ed., Hendrickson, 2010), 2:403.

and fasting acts as a turbocharger.[3] Other times, a particular need of mine or someone else arises, and I set a date on the calendar to petition the Lord with fasting.

A key point in considering your rhythms is to seek the Spirit's guidance. Ask him for wisdom to fast in a way that reminds you that God is better than food while also not losing sight of God's goodness in giving us food to enjoy. Ask him to prompt you in times of need and in seasons when regular fasting would be beneficial. In everything, ask him to help you look beyond practicalities and simply draw near to Christ through fasting and prayer.

Reflection Questions

1. What issue or need do you feel most urgency to fast and pray about?

2. Using the ideas in this chapter, create a plan for how you'll make that happen in the coming weeks.

3 Paul E. Miller, *A Praying Church: Becoming a People of Hope in a Discouraging World* (Crossway, 2023), 244.

5

Fast with God's People

FOUR FRIENDS GATHER in a Baptist pastor's study in 1788. Despite the ridicule and opposition they face because of their passion for world missions, they're determined to do God's will. These men read aloud the Pastoral Epistles and theological books. They seek the Lord with fasting, crying out for him to work in their hearts and in the wider church. And they go on to change the world.[1]

Across the centuries, God's people have fasted together to desperately seek their Lord. Against Satan's

1 Iain H. Murray, *The Puritan Hope: Revival and the Interpretation of Prophecy* (Banner of Truth, 2017), 156.

onslaughts, crushing persecution, pervasive plagues, and spiritual stagnancy, they have fasted in order to stand fast in Christ.

Individual and Communal

For most of this booklet, we've talked about fasting as an important discipline that helps us draw near to Christ and dwell in his presence (Ps. 27:4). It's right to do this individually, personally, and secretly.

But we ought to be careful about our spiritual disciplines becoming too individualistic. In our modern age, means of grace can become habits we try to optimize to reach spiritual fulfillment. Yet our disciplines actually tie us to something bigger than ourselves. Christians have been saved into a family, the church. In our local church gatherings, we come together to hear the word taught, respond to God in prayer, and sing his praises. Couldn't fasting be another way we join with others in prayer and petition?

By fasting communally, we join with our brothers and sisters throughout the millennia who have come together to bring their aching stomachs and hungry hearts to the Lord. We're also spurred on through the pain by knowing others around us are doing the same—we're not alone in our discomfort and pleading.

When to Fast with Others

What needs do you see in your congregation and the wider church? In society? In the world? Imagine how eagerly we could pursue all these needs in prayer with fasting as an aid.

Pray in a Time of Crisis

Along with their confession of faith and catechisms, the Westminster divines wrote the Directory for the Publick Worship of God. One section on fasting declares it a duty God expects from his people when judgment is inflicted on them or when they seek a special blessing.[2]

Likewise, John Calvin called for pastors to urge a churchwide fast when "pestilence, or famine, or

2 Directory for the Publick Worship of God (London, 1644), "Of Publick Solemn Fasting," Westminster Standard, https://thewestminsterstandard.org/.

war begins to rage."[3] We can gather to intercede in a special way when calamities come on us or on our world. Or, as a local church, you can fast and pray over crises closer to home: a member's diagnosis, the congregation's financial difficulties, or division and conflict within the church.

Pray for Revival

Historian Iain Murray offers this definition of revival: "An outpouring of the Holy Spirit, brought about by the intercession of Christ, resulting in a new degree of life in the churches and a widespread movement of grace among the unconverted."[4]

Throughout church history, revivals have often come out of seasons of earnest, even desperate prayer—at times accompanied by fasting.[5] Yet we

3 John Calvin, *Institutes of the Christian Religion*, ed. John T. McNeill, trans. Ford Lewis Battles, vol. 2 (Westminster John Knox, 2011), 4.12.17.

4 Iain H. Murray, *Pentecost—Today? The Biblical Basis for Understanding Revival* (Banner of Truth, 2021), 23–24.

5 For more on the history of fasting and revival, see chap. 5 in John Piper, *A Hunger for God: Desiring God Through Fasting and Prayer* (Crossway, 1997).

should be careful not to think that fasting is the "key" to revival, as though we make it happen ourselves or twist God's arm by our fasting.[6] Perhaps if you feel compelled to fast with your church, God intends to use it to further humble your congregation and make you receptive to an outpouring of the Spirit.

Pray for Your Hearts

The group I mentioned in this chapter's opening knew the needs of not only the global church but also their own hearts. One of them, John Ryland, wrote of their gathering, "Our chief design was to implore a revival of the power of godliness in our own souls, in the Churches, and in the Church at large."[7]

Four years later, these men were all central to forming the Baptist Missionary Society.[8] One of the group, William Carey, later sailed to India as a missionary. He translated the full Bible into six Indian languages and portions of the Bible into another

6 Piper, *A Hunger for God*, 116. For a discussion of the role of prayer in revivals, see Murray, *Pentecost—Today?*, 64–69.

7 Quoted in Murray, *The Puritan Hope*, 156.

8 Murray, *The Puritan Hope*, 147–48.

twenty-nine dialects. He also advanced Indian education, fought for social reform, and set an example for modern mission work.[9] All this came out of a heart fired with love for God. How might earnest fasting with a few godly friends change your hearts?

Pray for Anything Else God Lays on Your Heart

Gather with your church, your family, or Christian friends, and pray all kinds of petitions commended in Scripture. Pray for the lost in your community. Pray for the fruit of the Spirit to be increasingly evident in your congregation's life. Pray for the world's unreached people. Pray for the persecuted church. Pray for a crowded prayer meeting. Pray for discernment as you call new pastors. Whatever your local congregation—or your family, or your believing friends—needs, come together, fast, and seek the Lord's face. Let your hunger "put an edge upon [your] devout affections."[10]

9 *Britannica*, "William Carey," last updated August 13, 2024, https://www.britannica.com/.

10 Matthew Henry, *Commentary on the Whole Bible*, vol. 4, *Isaiah to Malachi* (Christian Classics Ethereal Library, 2003), on Zech. 7:1–7, https://www.ccel.org/.

There is great benefit in fasting alone, and Scripture teaches us that secret fasting is often the best path. But Scripture and church history also demonstrate the power of a praying group, and fasting can be an aid. We need so much help from God. Let's ask him together.

Reflection Questions

1. What potential benefits of fasting and praying with others do you see? Who is one person you could ask to fast with you?

2. What is one thing from this booklet that has changed the way you think about fasting?

3. What is one thing from this booklet that you would like to put into regular practice?

Conclusion

YOU LIKELY HAVE constant demands on your time and energy. Every corner of your life is stuffed—you have friendships to attend to, work to complete, meals to cook, ministries to serve in, clothes to wash, a husband or housemates to love, children to nurture, or taxes to file. It never ends. And the world around us calls us to do it all at once and perfectly. Keep improving. Pick up another side hustle. Organize more fun activities for your kids.

Our productivity culture demands strength. But we don't have it, and you know it, even as you keep running on the treadmill of *more*. So consider another way. In a world that extols strength, embrace weakness. Stop trying to be and have it all; instead, look to the God who is "over all and through all and in all" (Eph. 4:6).

Prayer is a means of admitting our weakness and asking God to exercise his strength on our behalf. By fasting, we express our prayers with greater humility, dependence, and desperation. It's not a burden meant to make us miserable. It's not a way to boost our reputation with God or others. Rather, it frees us to pray earnestly to our all-sufficient, merciful Lord.

This spiritual discipline is only for a little while. One day, the time for fasting will come to an end. Our Lord Jesus will return and usher us into the wedding supper of the Lamb (Rev. 19:6–7). We'll be full to the brim with Christ and have no longing left to express by fasting.

Until then, let's ask God to intensify our longings for him through fasting and prayer. Let's ask him to answer our longings to see the sin in our hearts eradicated and the evil in the world subdued.

Don't look only to the tangible outcomes of prayers to assess whether or not fasting "works." Look at your heart. If nothing in your outward circumstances changes but you depend on God more, fasting has done its work. More than anything, we should see fasting and prayer as a way to dwell more closely with our God.

The preface to this booklet series invites us to "taste and see that the LORD is good" (Ps. 34:8). Fasting helps us indulge our appetite for God by temporarily denying our bodily appetites. As our tastebuds and stomachs are deprived of the usual pleasure that food brings, we're able to savor the Lord in a new way. Our fast becomes a feast.

Recommended Resources

Dillehay, Tilly. "Awakening Appetite: Fasting as a Spiritual Practice." Chap. 9 in *Broken Bread: How to Stop Using Food and Fear to Fill Spiritual Hunger*. Harvest House, 2020.

Dillehay encourages fasting by presenting six compelling benefits of the practice.

Edwards, Jonathan. *Thoughts on the Revival of Religion in New England*. In *The Works of Jonathan Edwards*. Edited by Edward Hickman. Vol. 1. Banner of Truth, 1974.

Edwards, an eighteenth-century pastor and theologian, exhorted Christians to fast and pray (both communally and individually) in the hope of God bringing spiritual awakening and greater devotion among his people. Edwards's works are also available online at https://edwards.yale.edu.

Hyde, Daniel R. *Why Should I Fast?* Cultivating Biblical Godliness. Reformation Heritage, 2015.

Hyde mostly focuses on examples from Scripture and church history to build a case for fasting, but he also gives helpful advice on the practicalities.

Mathis, David. "Sharpen Your Affections with Fasting." Chap. 10 in *Habits of Grace: Enjoying Jesus Through the Spiritual Disciplines*. Crossway, 2016.

Mathis's excellent introduction to various means of grace has a chapter on fasting focusing on how it helps us express love and worship to God.

Miller, Paul E. "Turbocharging Our Prayers." Chap. 25 in *A Praying Church: Becoming a People of Hope in a Discouraging World*. Crossway, 2023.

In the context of a book about prayer, Miller presents an easy-to-read introduction to fasting, including the biblical background, benefits, and practicalities.

Piper, John. *A Hunger for God: Desiring God Through Fasting and Prayer*. Crossway, 1997.

This is my favorite comprehensive book on fasting and prayer. Piper includes an appendix of quotes about fasting from other sources, so it's also a great place to find further reading.

TGC THE GOSPEL COALITION

The Gospel Coalition (TGC) exists to renew and unify the contemporary church in the ancient gospel by declaring, defending, and applying the good news of Jesus to all of life.

Guided by a Council of more than 40 pastors in the Reformed tradition, TGC seeks to foster a mighty movement of spiritual renewal. We want to see God bless local churches with a gospel-centered ministry that fully integrates corporate worship, expository preaching, joyful obedience to God's Word, effective evangelism, loving community, and faithful engagement in the world.

Through its women's initiatives, TGC aims to equip, connect, and encourage women's ministry leaders and women in local churches globally. We do this through in-person gatherings and by producing resources including Bible studies, articles, podcasts, cohorts, books, and curricula. We support the growth of women in faithfully studying and sharing the Scriptures, in actively loving and serving the church, and in spreading the gospel of Jesus Christ in all their callings.

Join us by visiting TGC.org so you can be equipped to love God with all your heart, soul, mind, and strength, and to love your neighbor as yourself.

TGC.org

The Disciplines of Devotion Series

For more information, visit **crossway.org**.